Today is this...

poem shapes
and
word knots

from the
Multicolored
Universe

— TsdG

@toddymanners

this
——o ——o —— o ——
my poems and moments began
asking, then insisting, that
I maintain personal integrity
and do the next right thing,
for them. They knew,
and still do, that
this book must be;
saying "you have a responsibility,
to us."
Knowing that's true, for any
LGBTQs experiencing
spiritual abuse,
invisible mental health issues, and
so much unseen beauty.
All of this telling me
YOU-HAVE- NO-CHOICE
but to tell our stories
with your writing. 11724

——————

for Shadrach

Table of Contents

stem

Sky
   that makes your
   eyes taste sugar.
Sounds
   that make your
   ears breathe deeper.
Motion
   that you feel.

Summer 1990

50 cents or 75 cents

Two homemade donuts,
from a child's re-purposed
carboard box,
carried door-to-door
through the rain.

The tag-punched pay
for one bucketful
of orchard cherries;
hand-picked,
while climbing
through the delicious middles of
Heaven's belt loops.

Time-on-the-clock allowed
for one
three-hundred yard line
to be dug, three inches deep
through the rich smell of farm-tilled
earth; feeling
the heat of a pocketful of seeds,
at fourteen, learning that
some things are worth writing.

— — — — —

Commission received
from one
shadowbox key-ring portrait,
captured by Robin Hood,
chain-mailed, smiling, and shirtless
during a beautiful day
at Venice Beach.

The appoximate amount of
change created from one poem;
the first one, found
in my pocket-sized book
carrying
eight lines
of finding
this moment,
and this moment, and
this.

42423

Alex Hinton Cuba

Thank you for reminding me
about your cracked rib,
when my
brotherhood-hug
would not let you go;
wanting to be sure of you
knowing my years of gratitude
for every moment of
talent and
love you put
into my skin with your ink,
as you welcomed the rest of me
home.

　　...Finding out that
in Outer Darkness,
　we are the light...

92123
☺

Along Came a Big Fairy

Invisible, at first...
the protection from knowing
how laughter
sometimes
comes from hatred
helps children to believe that
laughter is just laughter
that's fun,
for awhile. Laughter
that's meant as a weapon
takes longer
to grasp for a child,
until their heart is choked
into understanding
the difference.
Finding out for the first time
that once upon a time
there was a benevolent enchantment
of protection
so manifestly in place as
to become invisible,
the way of warmth
only being noticed
once it's gone.

- - - - -

6

For a born fairy,
a basketball is a foreign animal
compared to a barbie-doll, although
every concerned person gives gods
unbridled guidence,
along with generous handfuls
of salvation candy;
doing their best to reshape
thoughts of which toys should
and should definitely not
be held close.
Eventually, finding that
all of those
toy-experty-people
become weary of so much confusion, and
the fun kind of laughter
further ripens.
Those too-sweet blue-eyed fairy-boys
get transformed
into faggots
who get pummeled
on the homo-boy choo-choo train
ho-ho-ho.
And, while we're doing all of this, you know,
soul searching,
who caused this
Monstrous Mistake
here, standing in front of us, anyway?

The beginning
of all that was,
and is
trustworthy,
going

through previously
unthought-of
rewrites
and,

the long-rotten laughter,
its piñata filled with
pretend salvation,
being the one
that gets smashed opened

and kicked
into bullshit's
soggy old ditch.

already valid

the first thing that I ever did
that was valid
was only
to get attention.

you can stop looking now.

Arterial Puppy Tail

That rhythmic thumping
across my back
left me mystified, at first;
thwap thwap thwapping
until the "oh, yeah" connection
was finally made in my brain.
The smiling puppy's happy body
tucked beneath my arm
as I carry her to the play yard,
without her ever wondering
about things like how and why
I am still alive,
even as her wagging tail,
smacking across my back
with happiness,
provides the reason.

Bones

Go straight to the End-scene
of somebody's home,
once it has been devoured by
    a roaring house-fire that has brought
    everything down; ground to powdery ash,
just like that.
Or, go to another home, and see what you see
after you're done hugging tightly to the
        bark of a thick-muscled tree with
both of your little-people feet   tugged all
                upside-down-you now
            over-your-head,   thrust into
        a life-sucking   tornado.
Or, even better again,
Visit a whole neighborhood of homes,
    after a third, fourth, fifth, or sixth
    whip-the-snot-out-of-you hurricane;
Nature, having her best time,
while brushing the day's knots from her hair.
Only then,
    when all of that is done, go see
        what is left. All spread out nicely
            on earth's green and blue tablecloths
covered in black crumble, garbagey water,
and surrounded by so many
        freshly detached
                        car doors,

will be nothing
    but

— — — — —

bare
naked
fireplaces;
exposed.
their bones,
secure
with a
purpose
even after

the whole house is gone.

When everything that
mattered
gets "act-of-god" flattened,
you have
opportunity
to find
that one,
immovable fireplace

standing.
ready
to continue
being
exactly
everything
it was,
created for
at the start.

— — — — — —

My own fireplace
still here;

intact,
my
love.

born from necessity

I am working today
to pay for
my final two
tattoos;

born from necessity,
just like the
thirty-seven tattoos
born before them.

Boxing Coach

My nervous system's boxing coach is here,
standing at the ringside of my bed
with his flattened hand hard-slapping
the canvas mat that I am
lying on; sideways eyes
swollen halfway shut,
halfway opened,
sleeping hands
wanting
to be left
tucked beneath my pillowed head,
legs bent at the knees in their
broken scissor shapes, my mind...
busy with counting the beats...
of that palm-slapping rhythm...
odd,
what that insistent coach-voice,
knowing way better than me,
yells through the loosening sleep as I reach
for my pen to
Stay Down! Stay Down! Stay Down!
All of that poetry
slapping my sleep into
breaches; my head swimming
through mobs of viscous shapes
begging for definition
too damn early.

Arms up,
    holding both
paper and pen;
    wily about
defying good sense again,
        ready
    for the horizontal-vertical
of another
    knockout round.

The Burning Sphincter

Not punching an asshole
squarely in the face when he
really...
really...
really deserves it,
is doing something
other
than just
letting him
get away with it;
maybe something more healing
in the long term,
for both of you.

Then again,
sometimes,
you've really just gotta

go ahead,

and
smash that motherfucker in the face.

Butterflies and Turkey Butts

Not to make any excuses, but,
turkey butt,
poems, to be all floaty-in-the-moment about it,
can be as fleeting as migrating butterflies,
for real,
and
if you're not already standing
in exactly the right moment
with paper, a fresh pen, and a butterfly net,
they'll be

    s p l e n d i f o r o u s l y
             b e a u t i f u l

right before you,
glowing with magnificent sunlight,
but...turkey butt...
the very moment you insert another
    thought about anything,
        they'll take off;
          leaving your poem

unpoemed
and you,
becoming
a turkey butt dweller,
who is only making excuses
again.

capture

deep, rich black
indigo
cobalt
cornflower
periwinkle
in all of their
sound
shape
and taste.

caught- up

Riding the red-eye
   on a sweet flight-of-ideas
      and only catching that lucky flight
after making a mad-sprint through
twelve labyrinths of terminals
filled with blind verticals eating their
crackly-wrapped slow-snacks.

How am I
now mind-tackled, strapped down, and
   ruefully butt-stuck again
      in another fucking free-fall. Dammit,
here comes the hallucinogenic splashdown,
left splattered and forced into
   squared-off rounds with understanding
      doctors throwing handfuls of
         psychogenic croutons
high
into the reliable wind;
carrying immutable sustenance
directly to the beaks of hungry,
ill-defined birds.
Rest assured,
some among us
prefer living in the hunger found
inside of our own floating playgrounds,

- - - - -

left unstrapped while we tackle our
three-dimensional puzzlesquiggles; gone
all saucer-eyed now
with a gyroscope's magnetized glide of
rotations through individualized
free-range parts.
Look.
Everyone else is bent into leaning, just
squeaking between their
             barely missed sequences of
unimportant events, and us, living here; being
baptized by the mid-air immersion of
all
five
shimmering
sensations while
finding our purpose in the cockpit;
                   our windshield wipers
     intentionally left
   switched off.

circled and spit at
while silent-walking home;
the emptied-out school bus kids
all enthusiastic about their spitting
at some grown-up's disgusting
eight year old. Then, stopping in unison;
standing with eyes blazing and
beating the living
shit out of whosiwhatsis in
his own stinkin' backyard. happy, when
his boohoo-boogers
began gushing down
right in front of everyone.
the registration of inner rage, smiling
at having its transactions
successfully wired
and fully transferred
into all of the correct accounts.
to be left alone with
the greatest childhood lesson,
now learned.
telling no one.
a kid's empty penance having its first
   happy birthday.
born today
from no longer being afraid of losing
everything;
clear,
that there was nothing there
to begin with.
being eight.

Uh-oh, Manie

The day after my father was born
men were jumping out of windows
from

very

tall

buildings.

Five months before
my father stabbed himself to death
on his
sparkling clean
kitchen floor

MEN

WERE

jumping

from

their

windows

again.

Our own bearded Tevye,
  his arms raised up high
  in a happy dance routine
  through the living room, after
whistling us home from the front porch

♪ ♪ ♪ ♪

for family nights, mountain hikes, and
  making small wooden cars
  out of blocks, for countless
  pinewood derbies.
Sitting down long enough
  to make dad-sense out
  of fourth grade times-tables
and then
telling laughing-until-crying jokes
  for the twentieth time.

Now,

— — — — — —

with a blade pressed
    twice
        into his chest;
            no longer vertical,

just

                    s p i l l i n g...

Dad
10/28/29 - 2/11/02

daily ordinariness
coming from every pore,
going in every direction
from the moment you climb out of bed and onto
the day's mountain range, searching
for that one handhold
that matches the foothold that
you have settled on.
mapped to conquer this massive
    i s   o   s   c   e   l   e   s
today, with every
little finger wiggle
when suddenly, there,
staring you in the face are
cave walls openly begging;
glittery rocks
scattered in their doorways saying
please follow our
 paths of what
you didn't already know that you
sought.

deep thoughts don't
deserve
their bad reputation
especially since
the shallow ones
just
don't
wanna know shit.

don't
waste
your life;
especially for
a bigger
motherfucking paycheck.

drunk on top of that

capital-D drunk
and then more
dee-runk on top of that,
until well cooked
beyond
any point of time.

losing all meaning;
finally.
        gone.

Thanks God.

Echoes

—○—○—○—

words being nothing more than shapes
made by stringing
            other shapes
                        together
into DNA strands that understand
            carrying
who I am to who you are and us
knowing, by tying and untying word-knots,
we see each other, breathing
the rhythm of our
            heartbeats
with echoes sounding it out
from our own mountain tops;
   saying hello...
                hello...
                    hello...

Eulogy from the city cemetery

the wrecking ball swings
with grace, back and forth ...
a ballet on a silent pendulum

of welcome destruction,
crashing into concrete hospital
walls, then, bulldozers circle

like buzzards set for tussling
over the broken parts that
remain. Mom,

in her hospital bed next
to me, while
I sit in a windowsill

and watch
through thick glass feeling
something of comfort

from the crumbling concrete.
Mom's small dog resting
in the hospital bed with her,

— — — — —

her hand gently gliding
back and forth...
back and forth with soothing

reassurances for them both, found
while tracing paths through the
mesmerizing forests all along

her happily dozing puppy's back.
Another three story hospital wall
cracks, opens, and falls while still

watching..., remembering..., church
as a little kid born believing,
though, with each podium speech

sleep grew into its own crescendo,
and, once the sacrament had been
passed, having another sacrament

of his own, one of resting
the side of his head on
his mother's soft lap

— — — — —

while she gently glided her hand
back and forth... and
back and forth, across

his four year old shoulders and
back and forth...
back and forth...

back and forth like a metronome;
meditation for a four year old.
My mother. Now...

twisted-up rebar,
grounded
and gathered like scattered

homemade spaghetti
while
my mother and her puppy

rest together
in her hospital bed
next to me.

Evaporation & condensation

the evaporation and condensation of
today's experiences forming
raindrops of dreamwords in my sleep,
clogging my brain filters with letters
until I'm forced to wake up to breathe.
Spending every ounce contained
in this aging body, fighting with the
twelve hungry mouths of death;
pulled in by its laughter at my
determination to not give in. Finding
poetry helps old men preparing for
dying just as it helps young men
preparing for life.

The face of God,
burning sunspots into our retinas,
as the new day begins to rise.

false leadership comes
pre-assembled
with automatic throttlers
of relevant information
superglued to its earholes and its grimacing
corporate-line kissing
lips.
it's all standard equipment,
built into
the power structure.

Family Portrait

done with just being dusted,
the chandalier is dancing
...radiant through a 5.8
    earthquake...
hand-sculpted shapes
wired together all
        shaking out prisms
        like raindrops;
refracted light flying all around
the surrounding walls of
        a room suddenly grown
far too small.
        every
        complicated
gem
        shimmering
        with uncomplicated
        eagerness
        as one
            precious
tumbleweed
        of diamonds,
    exploding
        with
    beautiful
        life.

from,
Roger

May you
always
remember
the gentle
redemption
and comfort of
walking a blind
shelter dog
in his old age
as
he
leans
with
your
leg,
walking
slowly
together,
you here,
claimed
reliable; his trusted guide.

give what you love

discovering there's a temporary nature
connected
to what has been made-up
through stories of knocked-up virgins,
versions of half-truths mirroring
each other's
fractured images, the
serpents and holy-shills
all alike with their built-in requirements

for respect,
for reverance,
and for maybes.

the eternal importance of
doing things the right way,
the only way,
their way,
learned by the age of twenty
when

being excommunicated
by the only absolute, anointed truth
saying:

"nevermind, not you."

— — — — —

would
have
fucking
killed
me
if I had not already learned

somehow...

to give what I love
the respect of my
irreverent
pulse,
continuing.

_____ go in. _____ o _____
Don't you dare add one more annoying comma.
Just drop a period on it.
Done.
You get the picture.
It's time to move.
Not going to; gone.
Release the damn
gravity straps and vigorously freestyle
through that scent
you've been swimming in,
Those where-you're-supposed-to-be-pheremones
gave you their map and are telling you
FUCKING GO!

— gravy —

Please
do not ever let someone
convince you that
their bullshit is gravy,
even
if you really,
really really
want to
believe in
their whole
desperate ladle.

the greatest lesson
that I learned
growing up
was that it doesn't matter
whether or not
someone
likes me.

handwritten palm

Sometimes I write
words on the palm of my right hand
during the night,
making a sort of dream-fistula;
room for a one-word psalm,
in order to remember
what I need to remember
in the morning.

Waking
and looking for words
my sleep-hands caught
through the night;
something of such importance
that even my sleep-self
took notes.
One word, grabbed,
held onto and pulled from
the dreamworld to keep
for the morning.
This one, today,
a three-letter-scribble
through closed eyes:
        cry.
Reminding me
that I had been able to do that
when Dad died; telling me
that I am not a total monster.

— — — — —

Later, two puzzled people seeing
my opened handwritten hand,
accidentally;
looking right at that same word
still speaking there, faintly,
while I was working
in a hospital for the day.
One emergency department patient,
and one Chaplain;
both of them saw it
separately, then,
perhaps,
found their own silent meanings
for the dreamword
sleep-written
on the palm of my hand.

i have committed myself
to promising
to not kill myself, but
it is going to be difficult
to continue
to give a fuck.

I will be here,
until the very end
of the whole universe
and then,
I will carry
our sanctuary
to wherever
we fly around next.

I would like to bare my Testimony

Singing sacrament songs about
                  Jesus
can still make me cry; genuine,
with love for him. That is
how

              I know that he is
one of the good guys

Even when
so many who say
they have claimed him,
continue to be
such complete assholes.
Amen.

the improbable fireplant
growing to the surface
from the bottom of the ocean,
giving its middle finger
to what's not expected
from water's basic
understanding.
brave, fiery tendrils,
unwavering.
continuing
through every liquid appearance
of being cornered. once
thought built to be extinguishable.
yet, the fuck off
that could go without drowning;
born with what happens, instead.
spirit lit
   like a stained glass window
in the center of a cathedral,
honoring the holy
apocalypse.

In other words
—o— o — o —

My big brother
randomly calling me
to find out
what Grandpa's favorite beer was
is everything
that heaven promises.

121223

in the time before icicles,
or any such thing as memories,
my mother created them both out of
everything terrible
for her crying 2-year old.
Lifting me up,
to prop against her sturdy hip
when the snow,
which had also never existed,
had gone up past my knees,
threatening to freeze me,
or bury me,
or worse; now,
earth's only mother,
pointing my gaze
with the attentive aim of one finger,
at a whole long row of
transparent somethings
of such extraordinary b e a u t y...
l i t f r o m t h e i n s i d e...
w i t h m o r n i n g s u n l i g h t...
for the first time
in my 2-year old life
I knew the feeling
of not having words
matching that singular moment,
with Mom.

instead ___ ○ ___ ○ ___

That yellowing, too familiar
rolled-up newspaper, held in the fattened
heavy hand of self-doubt
has decreed
that every self-effacing criticism is all
completely true, steadied when
kept enforced through whacking
old rolled-up lies into everything.
The truth of what's actually true
left in fresh scraps
everyday; gone rotten.

That tap-tapping-tap, of every still-less-than,
rolled-up together and wrist-smacked against
the khaki'd leg of your sole owner;
    actual physical contact is
            no longer even needed
against the skin of a well-trained soul's
hidden shiver.
The sound, itself, activating armies
of resonance; echoes of every corrected behavior
through the loving
E V I S C E R A T I O N
    of truth;
because that is what's best
for both of us.

— — — — —

Rocks, bullshit scissors, and god's
   flocked wallpaper have lost interest
      in who wins
   at the end of the day,
leaving only one natural predator
      worthy
of bringing on complete
   I N C I N E R A T I O N;
the fattened hand and its bullshit newspaper
   becoming, let's say,
   less attached.
      Then... a proper burial.

Tappity-tap-tap...   tap...

      now,

            only one more "here boy"
         from the glorious
         face-ripping tackle

to black.

irreverently,
disquietly
harshly now I scream at thee.
irreverently,
disquietly
fucking with your shushing
     as you plead with me.
irreverently,
disquietly
bowing my head
upwards,
to bite.
done with vascillating
     between
          begging and behaving
now,
laying you down
     to sleep.

It never starts with a smile when
sliding through the obnoxious,
necessary shapes, left all around
everywhere,
all unmatched,
all up and down; hundreds of tasks
labeled will-this-ever-be-done, then,
    something
      of such

          exquisite and
        unanticipated beauty

disassembles all meaning
of when. Appearing right through the middle;
her bare forearm
pressing the stem of an opened umbrella
to her chest.
Her hand,
    earth tones
holding white glass;
a scalloped bowl
from Mexico.
Beautiful,
   this woman,
     with herself...

standing in the rain
   offering sliced apples
     to a small circle of pregnant deer
       quietly assembling in front of her.

Kevin said that if I ever
got a tattoo of his name
with a heart around it,
or something stupid like that,
to just write the word "left"
right after it. But,
he never said that I couldn't
write a love poem
about him.
I love you, Kevin
Too gooey.
I know.
Not sorry. I would
love
to draw a heart
at the end of this
poem, but
I know that would
be pushing it.

♥

Lightbulbed

I used to think that
there was, maybe,
really
something wrong with me.
but, it turns out that
my brain just fizzes
with poetry.

Love.
—o——o——o——

Feeding the love you were born with
takes courage;
Living out loud around
people who hate what they
won't understand,
what does not fit neatly into
their imagined sacred
boxes, instead,
left out.
left scary.

But,
Pay Attention to This Part:

Not Feeding Your Love
Kills it.
Kills it the kind of dead
that doesn't scare people
because suddenly,
it actually does fit quite nicely after all,
right
into
your body's
dirt box.

— — — — —

Just read the Bible and you'll see,
they say,
let's read it together,
in chapter 200 verse 203:

Jesus smirked,
"That's what you get
when you choose
that lifestyle."

See?
That's not the way that it's supposed to be!
It's right here in black and white
(in the church-approved KJV)
highlighted with holy emphasis
between all of those loaves and fishes.

Hey, guess what.
Here's a cute little poem about that:

— — — — —

Fuck Them And Their Fucked Up Fears About Love
Knock their bullshit DOWN
and REMEMBER,
No Measurement by cardboard prophets,
with their 501(c)(3) manufactured redemption,
is worth
a single drop of blood
through sacrificing
your love at the alter of
their corporate gods.
not
one
single
drop
of your
beautiful
love,
spilled.
Not one drop.

Promise me
This.
And I,
also.
promise,
my unspilled love
in return.

low growl

when a dog low-growls,
close, in the invisibleness of dark,
you listen
in a different way; receiving
the warning like a deep undertow
through prickled skin and
spring-loaded eyes
double-wide with earnestness,
ear peripherals
spinning
in wild rotation.

magic isn't
only something for
ten year old boys,
finding hidden coins
behind the endearing
gullible ears
of grown-ups. Look
more closely
this time,
while
what appears
to be something
so-seen-before
mundane
works
its deft sleight-of-hand
showing that the trick,
of all magic,
is hidden
within
the minutiae.

making it rain

That bright green stand-up piano
used to be plain, flat
worn-out brown when we borrowed it;
wet now,
brought to solid life with all of her notes inside
playing
a perfect range of unapologetic raindrops
through her bright green leaves.
Drew and me, both
smeared with fresh paint
across our green foreheads and elbows
like we'd been growing
our own leaves,
sitting on the floor, laughing
"Look at my arms!"
Two newly born sprouts;
proud of our treehouse piano and
making it rain
together.

moments of noticing

the routines,
of well-balanced meals and regular showers,
being the first to ~~take off~~; just running out.
the front door has gone missing after
slapping the ass of what's-sensible, when it
   started making threats
to never come ~~back~~
while there are any of those damn
favorite pens and so-precious slips of paper
left anywhere
in this goddam house. next,
the pocket-knifed whittling begins;
chips of sleep in flurries
falling to the floor from both ends.
waking up,
never early enough,
with the most insistent words
ever written
sleep-scribbled;
every heart-powered flower captured,
blossoming right
across the palm's deep-sleep while
facing a rematch;
the headstrong poetry warrior
brandishing his cherished weapon,
with both eyes closed. his handwriting,
caught
wondering

in unreadable rhythms of multicolored marbles
making lip-smacking sounds as they roll
    through all of life's
tardive dyskinesia. yes, there is
zero time left for scooping the
  overflowing internal stimuli
from tenuous tennis-shoe'd footholds before
squashing the shoo-backs into flat tires and
grabbing the locked car door while
volumes
of frozen juice concentrate cans
hang
from your dangling tongue.
your favorite pen;
capped.

121923

Motorcycle meditation

Put your helmet on, if you want to.
We can start with 7th street
to the 710,
if we begin in Long Beach,
    t h e n ,   g o i n g
on a macaroni-necklace ride to
the 5 to
the 101 to
the 405 to
the 10 to
the 110 and then,
to the crown jewel,
best at night,
riding across the
Vincent Thomas bridge
back into Long Beach.
We can split traffic,
    when things get busy,
    just keep your legs nicely tucked-in.
How many numbers those freeways total;
who knows?
The right amount.

— — — — —

For variation,
if you're a guy that I'd like
to make out with,
we can ride to the top of
Mulholland Drive where
you'd likely say that
I've taken guys there before,
and you would be right:
having been taken there, myself,
    once upon a time,
by another guy on his motorcycle
showing me that same lookout spot.

If you're riding on your own, which is always
the best way to ride, go
    down Sunset Boulevard,
        starting in Hollywood,
late to the point of no cars left
    and   all   green   lights
all the winding-way to Malibu Beach.
Stop at the Hollywood Denny's,
if it's still there and you're hungry,
for a grilled cheese sandwich and
a cup of hot coffee, then
leave with your front pockets
    full of
        paper-napkin poetry.

My Beautiful Soledad

All of those monochromatic meteors
living on predestined
trajectories of missing
or not missing hundreds of
daily collisions while
here, in the tireless entirety
that already is and is never
either finished or unfinished, or
ever spending even one moment
of thought
of whether or not
this needed to be,
is
the already of always
flying together
hand-in-hand
while wearing our handmade
superhero capes,
all through our beautiful
and ever expanding
multicolored universe with
my Beautiful Soledad.

My little bit of heaven

It's impossible to think
that you left when you didn't leave
six non-existent years ago;
already and never ready happening
at the same time you are,
within the stillness here,
with me, breathing the beauty and
berating the no-such-things
every unshruggable day.

The nerve
       to think

anyone
would EVER
change
their mind
about ANY of it,
EVER EVER,
and still,

you,
going right ahead,

   with such GALL, and
      no SHAME; not to mention
         that awful DISTASTE.

   Standing
   TALL
   in front of everybody
      and
   Saying
      Right out Loud

— — — — — —

what
   polite society
      has established
("with over 2,000 years of tradition!")

is
NOT
to ever be
THOUGHT

   and especially
NOT

to ever
   actually be
      talked about,
(at least not in any
   pleasant ways)
and

You,
HERE,
(the unmentionable!)
saying you're gonna go on and just

– – – – – –

BE like that
ANYWAY?
No matter what ANYBODY says?

PROUD of it
Right Out Loud, my dear Lord
WHAT is this world
coming to?

The NERVE
to be...

followed by that
    Fresh,
heady aroma
of
their
neurotic
not-supposed-to-be topography
all mapped out and steaming
                    How
                    Dare
                    You?

Not News.

Nobody is listening
to Anybody because Everybody
talks in a blast over Everyone Else.
There is Nothing about Anything
that Anyone
can agree on. Nobody lets go
of their limb-fitted position-hammers,
all of those reliable Pullers and Pounders,
just Opposite Sides of the same head?
Who says?
Anybody could see more clearly, maybe,
if Someone could reasonably claim that
it isn't already too late
to save yourself by looking away
from the monetized train-wreck of a mess caught
in a constant hit-and-run
kept tumbling (together, at last!)
over a monster-cliff. The Perpetual Way
Everyday begins and
Everybody ends.
Plato's cave channel currently streaming,
with subscriptions being offered for only
two dollars extra, if you prefer
no commercial interruptions.
Act now.
(small print)

of lighthouses and imperfections

"if you don't do everything that it takes
to make it to heaven,
             then you really must not love
             your family enough
to want to be together with them
  in heaven again."
Mothers are imperfect lighthouses;
helping to steer their family
away from the invisible,
jagged shores of judgments damnation, because
families are supposed to be forever.
there, smiling, now
with a plate full of refreshments
and a warm greeting
        while listening
with precision and a mother's intensity
to the still, hollow voice inside
presenting its damning evidence
about her,
quietly believing
again and again, the condemnations met
    by measuring the lengths of every one
of her imperfections, then, finding herself
all tied-up with merit-badged boy scout knots
to God's
legendary
meatgrinder
of not
perfect enough.

of worth

it's easy
to say the cliché
that I am
my own
worst enemy,
but also
tragically
short-sighted
when I,
am
also,
my own gatekeeper.

People get stuck
on what parts go with what,
on which parts shouldn't go where,
and on all of the parts that should have been
left exactly
as they already were,

                        although

those were the parts that never fit anywhere
    to begin with.

It shouldn't all be so confusing, they say, because
Jesus already said where ALL of those parts
should and shouldn't go.
Simple as that.

                or

at least they believe that
the guy in charge at their church said that
King James said that
Paul, the mansplaining misogynist, said
that that one Jesus,
that he had never even met,
had said those things
    two thousand years ago,
and all of THAT,

somehow, still
makes people very angry
if everyone else doesn't also see it that way.

Hey Paul,
or Saul,
or whatever,
since you're already here,
I've got your tinkling bell.
It was buried beneath
all of those dusty thats and begats.
A useless brow-beater, anyway,
you, with your tinkling bell, speaking of charity
or love...
love!
(at least in the newly revised versions), while
everyone is already packing,
with only the right parts
getting stuffed
into each other's bags on the prayerful behalf
of everyone else's
forced rapture.

Pool Table

There's a new pool table
in the same place
where Mom's hospice bed
used to be.
A ceramic Santa is nearby,
holding a pool stick and a triangle;
offering a game with a smile.
Her new floral couch where I stayed put,
right next to her
as her body died,
has been replaced
with a new rowing machine.
The room has moved on,
faster than I did;
now, sitting here on the floor,
still breathing while
        holding the rest up.

Portfolio

People are successful at planning
their early retirements, while I'm busy
having an early
  resurrection.
You can ask every paper scrap,
stretched canvas, or lost
tchotchke, as they
sit, stand,
  or are stuck
to my brain's surface; a tattoo
from the past-present-future,
they will continue
to abide,
right where they're at
  with me, here
long after the third sunset has
hatched.

promissory note

realizing,
maybe for the first time,
that life
will
go on
without you.
all of love's promissory notes
will eventually stop crying.
left behind, to go back
to clipping toe nails,
trimming nose hair,
and cleaning the cat box as though
nothing
had ever happened
beyond
this.

A rabbit saved my life,
   at least once,
after she had been hit by
   some unknown
   in the middle of past-midnight.

When I stopped,
   after thinking about it for a little while,
   imagining, or not imagining that I saw
   her looking as though
   she was still alive, and then
having-to-turn-around, or not live with myself
   for not checking, because
   she was not moving; and who knows
when the next car would be coming
fast-around-the-corner
in the dark after me.

So I did,
   Turn around
And she did
   Save my life, after
I had helped
   To save hers.

— — — — — —

She was completely alive,
   but unable to move. Looking intact,
her eyes blinking at me from where she was
lying flat-out across the middle of
the road's slow lane.
I gently picked her up and took her home with me,
found a wildlife rehab,
and took her there
the next morning.

Seeing a fawn walking calmly through
the person's living room,
where I had taken my rabbit friend
to rehabilitate, reassured me
that I had found
the right help for her.

Two weeks later, after losing
babies that only her body knew had ever existed,
she was ready to be freed into the wild again
on the very same day that
      My-man-for-life,
                        or, at least
      for the previous eleven years,
left me empty.

— — — — —

Watching his exit that day,

reverse
down our driveway
from our living room window,

followed immediately by
a phone call to me from animal rehab
              and then driving
with the rehab guy
in a jeep,
            to a remote woodland,

my wild rabbit, riding alongside me
in a small dog carrier,
                         ready
to be hopping again...

RISE UP

When there is a need,
and there is a void,
there may
occaisionally be
a reason
for you to rise up.

Be ready.

RIVER

no matter
how many times and
multiples of
this-all-happening-before happen,
it's newly discovered
again, fresh,
in every single moment's
passing
as it happens.
I continue
to get carried away
by the strong,
swift
currents
found
in all of the rocky rhythms of
words...

11123 :)

_____. __roadtrip.__ _____

recording this
record breaking heat
with three new tattoos, like
beautiful body sweat
that won't evaporate;
here to remember
all the rest of our roadtrip
together.

The Root Sum

Although you can't see a tree,
or the ground that it grows from
literally smiling, if you
stop your body
and your thoughts
long enough to
Just... Be...There...
among them,
their smiles (when they're happy)
will pulsate all the way
through your soul.
Know how that feels
⟶ before ⟵
your time to go
gets underlined.

rub my feet
at the end of the day's boring parts.
we can talk about
some of the great things
we've been reading.
rub my feet
and we can talk about whatever
you want to talk about,
as long as it is
for a long time.
after that, you can
rub my feet
and you can say nothing
about anything
until I say so and like it
and, maybe then,
maybe once,
after months,
we could just
look at the lights
for awhile.

Seeing the Red Hot Chili Peppers play,
with only their tube socks on,
in '85

made me know
that I had found life

beyond
my Excommunication.

Shadrach

mine, for that mad dash you had
between repossessed,
naked drunkenness,
and being street-fucking
stolen; yours,
spent with me dashing
triple-amped between fresh
rejection and not yet
being willfully dead.
my legs wrapped around
the only presence worth knowing;
everyone praying for red lights and
us, running them anyway.
you stopped me from free-fall
with your 750ccs,
two fearless wheels,
and my borrowed dollars.
still alive.
still in your debt.
my Shadrach.

skipping a page

skipping a stone-heavy page from your story,
like a flat river-rock, bouncing
across a mirrored lake
sinking everything about
"that-one-time"

for good;
elbow cocked
with a fistful of

not
gonna
~~think~~
about
that

ever again,
then
sending it flying.

Bap! Bap! Bap! Bap!   Bap!

the surface not wanting it either,
until, after a breath, it relents;
swallows it whole in one gulp
leaving clusters of excited bubbles
chasing each other around
while it sways,
all the way
to the comfortable bottom.
finally,
not sunk.

slow dance

shadows gliding through
a friendly night breeze

carrying
gentle shapes

of comfortable trees seen

c a r e s s i n g
c o n t o u r s

of parked cars.
finding the wind's tempo just right,

their quiet slow dance,
unnoticed by others,
is
left

undisturbed.

wanting to write but not knowing what to write about?

Start with all five of your senses. Find a writing book and two pens and go through each of your senses, one-by-one, describing in detail everything that they're telling you, in exactly this place, in exactly this moment; right here and right now. Look around you and see what I'm talking about, with all five senses awake in this exact moment, no matter what and where that is. For me, here right now, sitting in a wooden guest chair that has one leg shorter than the others, giving the chair a decent rocking motion when I want it.

That's a good beginning... rocking, rocking, rocking, then, what to write next... the buzzing background sound of a television in another room, the volume low enough to not understand anything that anyone is saying, like hearing a fly that had been in front of a television for such a long time that the fly had learned how to sorta-speak human, buzzing on and on about fly-gossip and sugary treats in fly onomatopoeias. You get the idea. Go from wherever you are, in your own experience with right now... like, the right now of right where you are - right now.

Going through each of your senses like that, with your pen all scribblin', one-or-a-few of them will likely say "Hey! You stopped all of your busy-stuff for a minute! So, since you're here, noticing things, let's go on a mind-walk to the trailhead of this bunny path that you hadn't thought about for awhile." Follow that path to wherever it goes, and, hop-along to any other paths that you come across while you're on that one (being careful to hold your pen and your writing book steady as you hop-hop-hop... Hah!).

After that adventure, if you're still wondering about what to write about next, think of the day that you will die. More specifically, what is the-one-most-important-thing that you would want people to remember, or know, before you go bye-bye. Write that in as many pages as it takes. After you've written the first one of those, if you are still alive, write another, and another, and another before any of those moments also go away when you do.

When you've written about those moments and bunny paths for long enough, you will hear your own writing-voice saying "hello!" to you... what?! A writing-style all your own? Yes! You have one! Notice this moment and don't be scared, don't be rude, say hello right back! Be pals, you two! Then, go and tell a story together, starting with all five of your senses.

stay of execution

Who is the-one-being
you would
wrap yourself around,
to protect
with
your-everything
once everyone else
that you ever cared about
had been swept
far away; gone.
Here, looking at you now,
with wide eyes
wondering if you would
also allow that very last
don't-ever-let-go-of-me being,
be swept away
   like the rest.
Never gonna answer that evil kidnapper's
"let-go;"
death, prying away everything with its
cold finger-bones
draining
the warmth
from one side
of our bed.

stigma only wins
one
in a million
considerations,
and it has never won
through remaining
obedient,

and hidden.

stray

(written by a dog at the animal shelter)

it's ok if I never
find a home.
just feed me.
let your eyes
tell me that I'm
beautiful, and
don't kill me
while I'm waiting
to be found.

stray
(written by a young street hustler in Hollywood)

it's ok if I never
find a home.
just feed me.
let your eyes
tell me that I'm
beautiful, and
don't kill me
while I'm waiting
to be found.

SUBMERGE.—

it's ok to go someplace
on your own, letting yourself go
cry for awhile.
                    go for
     as long as it takes,
peeling away from EVERYBODY
for the cry of there's no tomorrow.
Let it go off the rails
in a place where you're not around
everyone else, avoiding bringing attention
to yourself among people
who are already very busy with their
     sorries and civilities... go somewhere
all alone, and let that overpowering grief
crack wide opened.

Nothing healthy is gained
by desperately trying to contain it.

It has got to merge with
  fucked-up reality;
face-down and
    huffing-in the wet,
         deep scent of earth.

Summer Extension

I couldn't have known that
we'd see each other, ever again, when
finding that you'd left,
on the same day that we met.
Who could blame you?
Us, sitting on top of a picnic table
in the city park, past dark,
drunk-crying and then suddenly, me
having to barf. There was no time left
for anything, even a pre-barfing kiss,
before blurting out my phone number
and running for cover around the corner
        to blurt out everything I'd had to drink.
By the time I'd returned, with
        both sides of my mouth wiped clean,
you were gone. Car and everything.
Who knew if you'd even remember my number
with nothing to write it on before I ran?
All that I knew about you was that
you were here for summer school,
I was probably 100% in love with you,
and that your name was John.

One whole month
of trying to forget about you later,
you called. Every one of my blood cells
recognized your voice
immediately.
Even through drunk-tears and me
     thick with liquor
you had remembered something
that we had done or said that had us
connected, now saying "yestowhatsnext," and

Motorcycle rides, everywhere.
Gliding through the curves
     of the Pasadena freeway
        at night,
           with no traffic,
              and your arms held around me;
us, pressed together, your head resting
on my back, more than anything,
is what I will never forget, including
doing the same thing
without wearing a stitch of clothing;
both of us butt-naked riding Shadrach
     on Friday night right down the middle
of Sunset Boulevard;
        purity in Hollywood.

— — — — —

Yelling to find the non-existent
"Claude! Claude!"
in-between singing
       Gilligan's Island on countless repeats
as loudly as we could, through the dust
  of a crowded ren-faire; finding out,
once having our fortunes read together,
that my biggest, most-hugest-of-all-wishes:
to be able to write until the very end of my life
   would come true.

"Those are not my shoes!" gang-planked
off of a cattle-boat to frustrated crowds waiting
with people-applause from the pier, and you;
staying anyway.
Too late for there to be anywhere else
to sleep, other than a few feet from the road
in a grassy ditch. Worth it,
to be naked again, watching island
   fireworks from a hill
        the next evening,
          away from the crowds and
            all of those cricked necks
while we fucked in the open air.

— — — — —

Laughing our asses all the way off
at the Hollywood Oki Dog,
on another picnic table, this time
in the middle of a jungle of potted trees
with you, making comical voice impressions
while eating pepperoni french fries, then
back to my painted treehouse apartment,
listening to music on cassette tapes and
 confessing that it would kill us
  if our mothers ever died.

Twenty years past losing track of each other,
after only one summer of our full-time
adventure;
the complete randomness, re-found
from over one thousand miles away.
You are here and me, here too, now
with my ant tattoo; d'Artagnon,
who'd been climbing up a ren-faire tree
as we'd leaned to the trunk
having our lunch together. d'Artagnon the
ant, inked forever onto my leg when we
both sorta left or,
   sorta did not leave after all; here,
still climbing.

Surprises

Serving as a full-time Mormon Missionary and loving all of it, then, surviving leaving Mormonism a year later.

Recognizing that there had been legit spiritual abuse, eventually, and letting go of the resulting self-torture.

Swimming into the ocean far-far-far enough to find myself with a whole pod of dolphins, all swimming around me; being caught-up in the epiphany to the point of forgetting that I eventually had to swim back!

Coming out to my family.

Shadrach.

Quitting a job that I hated, before looking for another job.

Going to Italy on a one-way ticket with $100, and staying for 4 months.

Getting sober.

Connecting with people, at all.

Bicycling 600 miles in 7 days, 5 times, with over 2,500 other cyclists; fighting AIDS.

Becoming independent.

Becoming a nurse.

Riding a train from Texas to play the "Red Hot Chili Peppers' song "Tear" on my banjo, while sitting on the ground right next to their brand new star on the Hollywood walk of fame.

Finding sanctuary.

Finding forgiveness for anyone who I swore I would never forgive, including myself.

Loving, and being loved by someone, for being exactly who we both are.

Marrying my Superhero Esposa for ETERNIDAD, and flying together through our beautiful and ever expanding Multicolored Universe. BESOS!

Understanding that $1 + 1 = 22$.

Writing this book.

Finding out
  that I am able to surprise myself,
    in good ways,
      more than once.

tall, tangled brush in the foreground,
dotted with daylight yellow flowers
spreading brightness through
   a brushy stick-maze, gazing
straight up at the sky.
wide stripes of earth's rich ingredients,
wet from the rain of two days ago,
reaching high with fist-sized stones
embedded through all twelve layers,
  their randomly scattered patterns on
  incline, like punched-through-paper notes
of a player-piano's
song-scroll. bared, winding roots
feeding generations of wild trees.
the glorious sunrise. being
greeted by a small rabbit, now
hopping out, looking at me, and wondering why
I had been standing
in front of her home
for such a long time.

11123 TBdG

dedicated to Erin

105

tears tumbling apart
and together,
bumping through newly found
gravity;
that homemade mixture
of inescapable sadness with the
unwritten, eternal poetry
of experienced joy.

the love of a son, insoluble,
    presently
        becoming confused
by all of the missing name tags

when everything says
                the same thing;

...my beautiful mother...

...my beautiful mother...

...my beautiful mother...

TEXAS

The first ice blossoms of winter
have bloomed, sunlight brightening
ice extrusions of movement through
long stems from last year's plant-life.
Now, tiny fireflies are
           already here,
                 the first few blinking
    in time to celebrate
earth's birthday; their friends all
joining in the neighborly rave; filling
tree-lined meadows with bobbing lights.
Cicadas arrive next; sound waves at
mesmerizing summer volumes,
      unheard for a year and never forgotten;
lost in rhythms inspiring dance
   moves of yellow,
                red, and orange,
                spread through
cathedrals of leaves, convincing
   any who have chosen to remain green
to join them, through the dance of
every moment, living in
           beautiful Texas.

Thank you,
zucchini
pear tomatoes
cherry tomatoes
giant green olive
grilled slice of red onion
artichoke heart
tomato chili dressing
pineapple chunks
cantaloupe chunks
and scattered confetti
of blueberries.
Thank you.

that can't be

none of the flower petals say
"he loves me not"
as each one
flutters
to the ground,
and still,
I cannot
believe it.

There's an equation in here somewhere

Letting a kid in a small town
grocery store have
a prolonged,
    straight-on gawk at you
as you walk by,
knowing that he may have
never
seen someone who
looked
like you
before; focused on
not returning his gaze
so that
he wouldn't be afraid,
and could continue to stare.
Smiling
at knowing
that mattered.

three earliers

at least three
earliers than early,
wake up and, before
even rubbing your
eyes, go very quietly
outside. now, while
standing still... wait
until you hear
the rhythmic sound
of trees singing;
your ears full
with their beautiful
night chorus.

today's nourishment is provided by
_____ ∘ ___purple___ ∘ _____

that bright purple mohawk, turned
into a mullet-y pony tail
springing out of
the back of your head
is looking like it belongs
to a five year-old girl; here,
seeing herself as a mermaid, ready
for any name-calling bullies, armed with
magic glitter and beautiful
sirena songs,
brave on her way
to first grade,
until seeing, wait...from the front,
those bright purple locks at the back
go with the face of a sixty year-old man
    with stony eyes that have seen enough
to know the complete freedom
of smiling sincerely, in return,
or knocking the spit and teeth out of
any jackass who tries to pull him back
into their ignorant bullshit.
same brave purple...

this one,
a purple blossom;
growing less tiny
through the fertile bed of
a cracked concrete
sidewalk

t
o
d
a
y,
in the glorious sunshine.

trauma knows
not to expose
its own backside.
so,
you can either
be patient with that,
or you can just
back
the fuck
off.

Two Poetry Missionaries
Knocking
        knocking
            knocking
for someone inside;
anyone, to come un-bar
your front door.
Bright earnest smiles,
standing shoulder to shoulder
in crisp white dress shirts,
proud of their ironing,
clean lines ready for the necessary
poetry-midwifery because
God is the muse who believes in you.
Sometimes they arrive
prepped with eighty-proof epidurals,
providing what can become
the only humane way for birthing
a poem that has breached.
Gently handing you a beautiful book
    filled with blank pages and promises;
    safe-shelter for bare-naked testimonies.
Your complicated mind finding
    prayed-for relief;
poem shapes becoming

stillness
within reach, then,
once again... here
the familiar poetry comes.
Shuddering
with Violent Urgency,
Desperate
for any Thirsty Paper while
Ripping the Stuck Cellophane from
Boxed-Up Pens
Made
Especially
for Containing
All of the Chunky Stuff... and Gunk.
God Save My Soul and
Please, bring me your Poetry Missionaries,
riding their bikes
with arms full of blank books
tucked like footballs
beneath the elbows of their
crisp missionary shirts, before
it's time for

another

baby.

Dad!

You cannot make your escape
that easily! This isn't
some fucking dine-and-dash!
You have got to pay!
You-have-not-died
(very long ago) so
there may still be time
to catch up with you!
Today!
I'll leave the how-of-that
to all of the others who are
in charge of such things.
All that I know how to do
is to get on my motorcycle
and chase you down.
Fuck the helmet.
I won't be needing it. In fact,
not having it will help me
to get to you faster.
No matter where you are,
or where you thought you were going,
I will find you,
and beat what's left of the holy
fucking shit out of you.
Go ahead and think you've escaped.

Oh...
    wait.
well then...
    shit.
This is absolutely the worst time for recovery
    to be reminding me that Now
would be a good time
to pull off of this freeway and
call
anybody.
The winning coin flip going with
Jack G.
for this time,
rather than the jackshit of another bottle
of JD
        or wild turkey,
                yes, I promise,
just for one motherfucking day,
  I will give up the holy
            mind bleeding chase
and not drink
all of my bloodthirsty rage;
today.

what should have been
anyone's murder to commit, but no,
of course it was by his own hand.
weaseling out again; gone
through his final escape... until,

— — — — —

several forgetful years of just-todays later...
seeing Dad while I was dreaming,
where he sat in the middle of the actual
Mormon Tabernacle Choir, although,
he was not joining their singing.
of course this was incredulous,
even for dreaming. Sad, though,
seeing him sitting all quiet like that;
saying to him,
Dad!
Why aren't you singing?
You have made it all the way to
the Mormon Tabernacle Choir!
He continued to sit, looking at me
for a moment before saying
I cannot sing until you've forgiven me.
I said, Dad!
I forgive you!
Stand up and SING!
At
no
point
since
then,
have I ever wanted
to chase him down,
 alive or otherwise, again.

119

Unclamping a becoming

Letting go of people
and pain
should be neither
impossibly difficult
nor the millionth iteration
of cliché. Regret,
floating away like a
helium balloon,
unstrung from
   what was
      never owned
            to beg

h

t

i

w

i

n

unwind
s t r e t c h
your arms and legs out
as far as they will extend;
heavy in bed then remain
still...
your man's-best-friend
sleep-breathing
uncomplicated dogdreams,
at home next to
your comfortable chest;
nothing less than
the great unwind of

d o n e
e n o u g h .

who writes for the people
who felt that
they didn't matter,
other than people
who were told
that they don't
and have chosen
the fact
that they're going to matter
anyway.

the worrying moors
always have available vacancies for
people just there with a drop-off
who end up staying
for permanent residencies;

looking for something of
what they've lost
while they're

wandering
and wondering about
what unholy unevenness
had even brought them there.

In case you were wondering
what it feels like
to experience straight-up

spiritual abuse...

your Soul
  gets
Pulped
  by
heaven's self-anointed
people of holiness
swinging their not-so-gently-used
  crosses, now re-purposed
    into wooden
        baseball bats splintering
with god's true love delivered
    through every whack
      of holy judgment
        to the sweet music of
          salvation's laughter.

— — — — —

any
leftover sludge is then
easily hosed-off
of guilt-free
church sidewalks.

there are no complicated questions.

god's people walk away,
  wrapped in warm quilts
    of re-imagined scriptures;
  their pockets, re-filled
with sacrament wafers.

Today is this...

How many people have out-survived
the hungry drains
of their own mental illness;
left alive after quietly
being ravaged by self-aimed
claims that there is no answer.
How many,
even or odd, is too many
years spent trying
to figure it out... and now, here,
too late or too close
to ever find any focus, again.
The problematic part of suicidal thinking
is the thinking,
and the re-thinking, about how
if-you-ever-told-anyone
of its subtle ginormity, like
          being strapped to a rocking chair,
vertiginous to the point of nausea
with the squeaking and squeaking,
that same weathered spot
filling your tired head, then
the-well-meaning-they
would immediately

- - - - -

try to stop you from doing it;
before you had the chance
to go through with
the stopping
yourself.

so...
    o b v i o u s l y
you don't want to say anything.
left for now,
for the more important work:
picking up the shattered parts
of what-wasn't-supposed-to-happen, then
    already lost
again, in
    another whirlpool of thought about how
god told me to fuck off
    in his superior "my ordained white men said so"
way,
right to my face — the voice of god
(just in case I hadn't been paying attention),
for long enough
    for me to hear
            my own
                disembodied voice
        e c h o i n g

— — — — —

the spiritual abuses of fucking false prophets.

finding my way back from that
        misdirected waste disposal,
    with a rusty shank
and no qualms
about
    who claims to own it;   now here
        being hand-delivered, with muscle
and a fuck off
of my own.

To say "there are no words"
    for holy blood-spilling maybes
is a cop-out with the best intentions;
    kindly delivering unknowable options
along with
    a Police Order of Emergency Detention.

Mental illness and mental heath are
the sorta-pals of
        a grasshopper
            jumping
                onto a
                springy flower.

- - - - - -

annoying each other,
just slightly,
while also asking:
how did those who lived
learn to matter again?

Ask the presumed guilty;
police-greased thumbprints
smudged and swirling
through finger-painted solar systems
on a dot-to-dot-path somewhere
between the constellations of
Satan's tassled pasties and god's
glittered pom-poms.

Sometimes,
people will get there.
Sometimes,
people won't. And
Sometimes,
saying it out loud will help.

Look for my greasy thumbprint
flying
right there next to yours.

— — — — —

I love you.
I am with you.
We can do this...

Introduction to
... Shapes...

At one of the first Lollapalooza music festivals that ever happened, I saw the band, Pearl Jam, playing outdoors during a glorious afternoon with two of my best, most beautiful friends ever in the whole world, Tony and Daniel. I was having one of the best fucking days of my entire life, when Eddie Vedder stopped singing for a moment, and asked "Is everyone having a great day?" Everyone yelled "YES!!!", with my own voice one of the loudest among them. "Have any of you also ever thought about killing yourself?" The crowd suddenly went quiet. "Yes, I have," I thought to myself; not daring to say it out loud, even to my great friends who were standing right there next to me. Then, he immediately said, "Doesn't a day like today make you glad that you didn't do it?" My reply was also immediate; my body feeling like it was glowing while I said "Fuck yeah", out loud this time. Having had that glad-to-be-alive moment pointed out to me, on that day, has stayed with me for thirty years.

The picture on the cover of this book, was taken on a fantastic morning that I got to experience, a few years after I had made the suicide attempt I wrote about in my poem "Today is this..." Now, "today is this..." had also become a morning of epiphanies, with a person who I would have never met; eternal in the beauty of that precise moment. The beautiful man in the photograph, Andrew King, lived for 35 human years and all of forever; inspiring me every day with his creativity, his intelligence, his humor, his refusals to ever filter himself for anyone, and his unapologetically pheromonal instincts, especially with my face buried deeply into his delicious armpits. Ok, that part you maybe didn't need to know about. Hah! In this photo, Drew is making it rain, while we sit together like kids on the floor, drinking espressos and smoking camel wide cigarettes. Making it rain has always been Drew's superpower. To this day, whenever it rains, I thank him for still being here, sharing the day with me wherever I am. Hearing any music by Cocteau Twins will bring him here the same way. Just look at my arms and you'll see.

The reason that I wanted to introduce my poem ...shapes... this way, is because Drew would always talk about the original "Blade Runner" movie, focused on incept dates and life spans and repeating, verbatim, the Tears in Rain poetry at the end of the movie. Drew was living with AIDS before it had become something as treatable as diabetes; a time when our entire community was left shredded. He didn't know how long he had left, his own version of "incept dates", but he was going to live ALL of it, fiercely independent the whole way, and he will remain one of my very favorite superheroes long after I stop breathing.

The movie "Wings of Desire", showing one character having a conversation with himself about all of the poetry of life he'd experienced, from the middle of a road after crashing on his motorcycle, and the movie "After Life", with its characters who had all recently died, deciding on their one, most-favorite memory to take with them into their next life, were also huge inspirations for my poem; these are the ...shapes... of my life making its own "Tears in Rain" moments, each one filled with the genuine gratitude of "doesn't a day like today make you glad that you didn't do it?"

... made eternal...
...the moment...
...they were born...

...shapes...

—— o —— o —— o ——

...homemade school lunches in brown bags, on the kitchen counter, each one containing a hand-written note, from Mom, for me to read while having my lunch...

...Mom showing me that monarch butterfly cocoons can sometimes be found on the beneath-side of milkweed leaves...

...Mom's homemade everything...

...walking with Mom through the narrow, cobblestone streets of Venice, Italy at night, with some of Drew's ashes in my pocket, on our way to a small church, to hear a string quartet...

...every one of my beautiful Soledad's drawings...

...out-of-state teenage-roadtrip with my best friend, Robb, betting on who would get laid first, and seeing "Heavy Metal" at the Cinerama Dome, in Hollywood...

...dancing all night long, with a whole room full of gay men...

...kissing someone, passionately, without first knowing either their name or the sound of their voice, because our eyes locked onto each other and said so...

— — — — — —

...naked with Michael in the bathtub, singing Carpenters songs together in our soapsuds on a Saturday afternoon (Raah!)...

...bit-nipple pain that sings into the next day...

...riding a borrowed jet ski along the Italian Riviera, jumping off and seeing Jesus Christ reaching his arms up from the bottom of the Mediterranean Sea; then, floating on the top deck of a midnight boat to Sardegna, lying flat on my back, perfectly alone, looking straight up at star-filled quiet...

...flying with my arms stretched out, over the bobbing heads of a pit full of concert goers, while wearing my blue denim dress...

...going to jail for Julie Andrews...

...Drew's homemade pizza, Kevin's homemade mac & cheese, and my beautiful Soledad's homemade calabacitas...

...living in the crescendo in Scotland...

— — — — —

...thought-vapors caught on index cards while driving...

...maintaining personal integrity and doing the next right thing...

...painting with music playing when words can't explain...

...Flea singing "Pea", especially the punk rock version, and Anthony Kiedis singing "Wet Sand"...

...Singing Bronski Beat's "Why?" out loud about kissing a man on the lips...

...Keith Haring...

...every tattoo and every motorcycle ride...

...Kevin's birthday party pie-fight, in the yard with all of our friends, followed by walking to the lake together so that we could all wash off; a small parade of us, still covered with pie...

— — — — — —

...the first firefly each spring, followed by the first baby deer...

...Dale Manzella...

...Matt saying "don't think that this isn't you"...

...singing "Fast Car" with Chris...

...double rainbow carpool with Chuck...

...booming thunderstorms...

...Roxy's cove...

...Kate, believing that one day I would write a book, when she was ten years old...

...Tricia's always thoughtful questions...

...Bethany's birthday basket of smiles...

...horseback riding on a beach in Mexico with Monica...

...climbing through art with Devon...

— — — — — —

...being superheroes of the multicolored universe with my Beautiful Soledad; us becoming Married (BESOS!) together barefoot at Venice Beach, then running up and down the shore holding hands, our superhero capes flying high...

... my beautiful Soledad holding my face with both of her hands when she kisses me...

... giving the tree-side funeral prayer for a bright yellow songbird, who I found after her body's life had left; then tattooing a picture of her on my hand so that she could keep on flying as I write...

— — — — —

...being a true missionary at nineteen;
proud to be wearing my suit while riding my
10-speed bicycle, scriptures secured to the
small rack behind my bike seat...

...now, decades later,
     with a purple mohawk; here,
          writing my own scriptures...

today

Thank you, God,
   for this new day.

Thank you
   for being right here with me,
   watching every sunrise,
   and riding, either front or back,
   on every motorcycle ride.

Thank you for this book,
   that only you,
   Drew,
   Kevin and Mom,
   and my beautiful Soledad knew
   I could write.

Thank you, God, for
   everyone in my happy animal family,
   from the very beginning;
   and for every one of our
   mutual rescues, being together.

— — — — — —

Thank you for not caring that I swear at you
on the days that make no fucking sense.

Thank you for showing me
how to feel gratitude
for all of the tiny
miraculous moments scattered
through every single day.

And thank you, God,
for my beautiful dog, Applejacks,
who I know will continue to stand
right next to me
and love me no matter what I write,
or do not write,
for forever; my best friend.

I love you, God.

Thank you for all of the everything
that has brought me here with you,
today...

ps,
these open pages that
I've left at the end of
my book are for you
to write your own

...shapes...

your own, eternal,
"Tears in Rain" moments;
yours to keep,
no matter what anyone says,
for forever...

...   ...

...   ...

Made in the USA
Monee, IL
11 September 2024

0d65111b-3e32-44ed-9483-3a487b03eae7R01